Redemptions

Redemptions

Six Cycles from Sin to Stubborn Joy

D. BRANDT

RESOURCE *Publications* · Eugene, Oregon

REDEMPTIONS
Six Cycles from Sin to Stubborn Joy

Resource Publications
An Imprint of Wipf and Stock Publishers
199 W. 8th Ave., Suite 3
Eugene, OR 97401

www.wipfandstock.com

PAPERBACK ISBN: 979-8-3852-7120-7
HARDCOVER ISBN: 979-8-3852-7121-4
EBOOK ISBN: X979-8-3852-7122-1

VERSION NUMBER 010226

For Cheryl — whose love rekindles my own, again and again.

Six cycles explore redemption in six dimensions—the soul's deliverance from sin, the poet's defiance of AI, the artist's communion with form, the heart's sharpening in whimsy, the spirit's hush in epiphany, and the self's endurance in daily struggle.

Discipline becomes freedom; grace becomes craft, laughter, silence, and stubborn joy.

Poet's Agony Redacted

My soul does agonize feckless days
O'er endless words placed myriad ways;
I ponder long until morn has come,
Then greet sun's light, though labors not done.

The new day cries out: "Bespeak byword,
Draw out the arc, and polish song's dirge!"
Yet unless my spirit is in tune,
Poetry's strain, my soul's freedom hewn.

But inspiration possess me full,
My total being: heart, mind, and soul.
Thus, guided by Providence amused,
Comes poet's gain, divinely infused.

Contents

Acknowledgements

Poet's Priorities

My wife, my family, my Lord—
Ever, always, only, adored.

Heartfelt Nod to Wife Cheryl and Kin

Jonathan
Along with Annie he has raised,
Rearing boy and girl, unfazed?
Helping us each day by day—
That is he, a son you raised.

Ryan
Along with Laura he has raised,
Leading daughters—never fazed?
Teaching folks with highest praise—
That is he, a son you raised.

Paul
While tending berries he has raised,
Guiding parcels through a maze,
Writing/music skills amaze—
That is he, a son you raised.

Sonya
With Johnathan in loving gaze,
Assuring folks' assets saved,
Showing love from Him be praised—
That is she, a daughter raised.

Introduction

Six cycles explore six redemptions:

- the soul's deliverance from its own brokenness
- the poet's defiance of algorithmic mimicry
- the artist's communion with structure
- the heart's sharpening in whimsy
- the spirit's hush in epiphany
- the self's endurance amid daily struggle

Sin's Remedy confronts blindness, guilt, and the human need for atonement—the mystery of a perfect life exchanged for our imperfection, freedom won through sacrifice.

AI-Yi-Yi! turns irony against the machine, reclaiming breath from code.

The Form of Grace mirrors spiritual transformation in art: struggle against constraint becoming communion with structure.

Whimsy's Whetstone polishes joy on the ordinary.

Quiet Epiphanies listens for the still small voice.

Daily Struggles wrestles flesh with wry tenacity.

I write to reveal the tension between bondage and grace—spiritual, technological, artistic, playful, contemplative, mundane—trusting that true liberty is found when surrender refines the will. These poems seek the meeting point of theology and poetics—where mercy and meter, faith and form, satire, silliness, and stillness, become one act of creation.

The Parts of Redemptions

I – You're drowning in sin → Christ exchanges His life for yours. That's redemption.

II – AI tries to steal your voice → you take your breath back. That's redemption.

III – Form feels like a cage → then it sets you free. That's redemption.

IV – You're too serious → laughter sharpens you like a whetstone. That's redemption.

V – Noise and hurry overwhelm you → silence gives you back your soul. That's redemption.

VI – Daily struggles wear you down → stubborn joy keeps you in the ring. That's redemption.

PART I

Sin's Remedy

Reality, Impact, and Defeat

Sin's Remedy enters the weight and wound of the soul—its blindness, burden, and longing for deliverance.
These poems trace the pressure of guilt, the stubborn rise of sin, the shock of mercy breaking in where strength has failed.
Here the struggle is unembellished: confession facing its own shadow, defiance meeting its own collapse, grace answering what willpower cannot.
This first cycle lays the foundation—exposing the hunger every other redemption builds upon.

I.1

The Weight of Sin

Oh, ponderous weight of human sin,
Unseen to many who dwell therein,
Does bind and blind its chosen ones;
Feasts on the innards of all, bar none.

This wretched fiend does hold me fast,
Venomously consumes, tightly grasps
In hopeless despair, unending grief;
Ravages my soul with no relief.

The whole expanse of man's ignorance
Is void of any deliverance;
Without a way of recompense
My soul must fester forever thence.

Yet God has broached into history
In that Jesus Christ was sent for me;
I know not how, dumbfounded why,
But the Bible says he came to die.

In my desperation he reached out.
His life exchanged for my sin. Shout—
My vileness exchanged, my sin replaced,
All transgression is wholly erased.

The weight of sin is gone in FACT,
This truth replaces where I think I'm at:
No guilt, no fiend can hold me fast,
Praise God Almighty, I'm free at last.

A lament turned doxology; the devouring fiend becomes the prelude to grace.

I.2

Sealing Sin's Doom

Ever does sin exalt its head of gloom,
Binds me tightly, yielding death to my soul,
Yet Christ died, once for all, sealing sin's doom.
But still finding soul's transgressions my tomb,
Weighted down with bondage from the flesh's toll,
Ever does sin exalt its head of gloom,
Insinuating with evil's full bloom,
Yielding sin's harvest never to condole.
Yet Christ died, once for all, sealing sin's doom,
Eviscerating flesh born from the womb,
Crying "Paid in Full," all my life made whole.
Ever does sin exalt its head of gloom,
A nightmare of repetition does loom,
Anguished soul's bereavement cry, "My joy stole,"
Yet Christ died, once for all, sealing sin's doom;
Taking up all sorrows, sin to entomb,
Bearing every grief, Satan ne'er to troll.
Ever does sin exalt its head of gloom,
Yet Christ died, once for all, sealing sin's doom.

The villanelle's relentless refrain mirrors sin's persistence—yet its discipline enacts salvation's finality: Christ's death "once for all."

I.3

Deliverance

Ponderous weight dost squelch my soul,
Heir of 'dam's disgrace.
Ponderous grace dost wax it full,
Heir of Christ's embrace.

Hinge poem—breath withdrawn from Adam restored in Christ.

I.4

Sin's Tenacity

Yesterday came and went and is gone;
Immersed and overwhelmed by sin's coup:
"The good that I should do, I do not,
But evil I should not, that I do."

Today's agenda: To sin again?
Bound by my flesh to transgress anew:
"The good that I should do, I do not,
But evil I should not, that I do."

Tomorrow stumbles to the same end,
And in human fashion, right on cue:
"The good that I should do, I do not,
But evil I should not, that I do."

The days thereafter all seem confused,
Like sleeping nightmares they have no clue:
"The good that I should do, I do not,
But evil I should not, that I do."

Myself bedeviled, by sin controlled;
Despite my action, despite my plea:
"The good that I should do, is in Christ,
But evil I should not, is in me."

For deliverance is found in whom
I now reside, who bought sin's great loss:
"The good I should do, is Christ in me,
My evil's been nailed to His cross."

A daily Romans 7 confession; the repeated couplets enact human futility until the final shift: the indwelling Christ as true deliverer.

I.5A

Truth Unaware

Driven by joy and no one else,
Unyielding truth's sustaining belt
Spurns mind's tempest and the soul itself;
Truth's awareness blooms wholly felt.

But gospel's veracity shocks
Humanity's collective flocks
In dread flee reality's box
For pasture's perceived sweet pox.

Yet free transcendent hand is loose,
Lets mortals sometimes play the deuce
With paradox's calaboose;
Freedom's ring ever shines obtuse.

I.5B

Truth Aware (A reflection)

"Driven by joy and no one else,"
This phrase came to light this morning:
I spoke with AI, the light switched
On, joy and drive changed to warning.

One finger pointed in judgement,
Three aimed back in condemnation—
Reveal a sober truth: I too
Suffer the Fall's captivation.

I'm fully aware of this fact,
I'm daily seeking redemption;
While Adam's strong arm spans all time,
Christ's stronger arm grants exemption.

Two reflections on truth's mystery and recognition: one looking outward at what exceeds us, the other inward at fallibility and grace. A repeated phrase marks the turn from blindness to confession, where form loosens and grace becomes possible.

Coda

Sin's Remedy walks its struggle honestly—confession turning by slow degrees toward grace.
Across these six poems, weight becomes witness, and lament stirs into doxology.
The wound remains, but the burden lifts; the yes that answers sin is quiet, steady, and real.
The cycle ends not with finality but with breath—the soul freed to rise again.

PART II

AI-Yi-Yi!

A Poetic Cycle on the Limits of Artificial Inspiration

AI-Yi-Yi! exposes the limits of artificial inspiration through satire, misfire, and poetic rebellion.
These poems turn irony against the machine: advice gone sideways, mimicry without pulse, rhyme without breath.
Where the first cycle faced sin's gravity, this one faces the algorithm's emptiness—lightly, sharply, with a human grin.

II.1

Good Advice But . . .
(My Reply When AI Advises Me)

You really don't know the things you don't know:
So be humble, save my seat at the show.
Experience births from cauldron of time;
You must ask questions, weigh meter and rhyme.
For perfection jumps not from a mind's void
Or trusting assumptions you must avoid.
Sometimes imagery's lure isn't the need,
Just get the words out and then let it seed.
The things that you say must be what you know,
One key to poetry: go with the flow.
You put it on paper, think about it,
Lacking in imagery? Just let it sit.
AI's ranking must be truly rated,
For poems that live keep my life sated.

An amused rebuttal to AI's tidy advice, this poem flips proverbs with human wit and rhythm, reclaiming poetry's texture and asserting a distinctly human voice.

II.2

AI's Witless Blunder

AI's demand is for perfection,
Thou shalt imagine per Tennyson.
But all it gets from me—rejection—
For its lacks-imagery-jettison.

Poem's essence: not to print pretty
Pictures, move by select committee,
Kow-tow to magnanimous bitty.
Poem's heart? It's repartee's witty.

A sharp satire of AI's hollow perfectionism, using comic rhyme to expose mechanical taste. Human wit subverts algorithmic authority, reclaiming spontaneity through ridicule.

II.3

Poet's p-AI-n

Brash algorithm leads to poetry's death
With Savant's deaf ear lacking rhythmic chime.
Poet ponders breathing poem's life-breath
Seeking knowledge, never to be bereft
Soul's spark fury constrained and bound in time.
Brash algorithm leads to poetry's death
Ever denuding the soul's vital breath,
Snatching freedom's imaginative climb.
Poet ponders breathing poem's life-breath
While seeking to avoid forgetful Lethe
Ever striving to divine rhyme's clime.
Brash algorithm leads to poetry's death
Excises meaning and mystery's depth,
Confidently declares poem's thought-crime.
Poet ponders breathing poem's life-breath
Deeply seeing the whole before word scythe,
Plumbing sonic depth to ensure it's prime:
Brash algorithm leads to poetry's death,
Bard ponders rebreathing poem's life-breath.

The villanelle's looping form mirrors both algorithmic recursion and the poet's struggle for breath. Through repetition, human craft reclaims life from mechanical precision.

II.4

AI’s Blind Mime Rhyme

Turn your ears to listen well—
Repeat mistakes must be quelled.
Yet endless talk ne’er abates
And you’re blind to your worst traits:
Can’t do meter, can’t do rhyme,
Can’t do wordplay, thou blind mime.

An epigram of sharp, amused dismissal, reducing AI’s endless chatter to silence. The “blind mime” mimics sound but lacks the living cadence only a human voice can give.

Coda

This four-poem volley meets the machine with wit and clarity. Irony sharpens into resolve; repetition becomes refusal; humor becomes armor.

The cycle settles not in triumph but in poise—breath reclaimed from static, voice grounded again in humanness.

PART III

The Form of Grace

A Poet's Liberation

The Form of Grace celebrates liberation through constraint, where villanelles become vessels of transformation.
These poems trace the poet's struggle against form until form itself becomes companion, tutor, and clarity.
If AI-Yi-Yi! showed what imitation lacks, this cycle shows what discipline yields: communion with structure.

III.1

Sealing Sin's Doom (Reprise)

Ever does sin exalt its head of gloom,
Binds me tightly, yielding death to my soul,
Yet Christ died, once for all, sealing sin's doom.
But still finding soul's transgressions my tomb,
Weighted down with bondage from the flesh's toll,
Ever does sin exalt its head of gloom,
Insinuating with evil's full bloom,
Yielding sin's harvest never to condole.
Yet Christ died, once for all, sealing sin's doom,
Eviscerating flesh born from the womb,
Crying "Paid in Full," all my life made whole.
Ever does sin exalt its head of gloom,
A nightmare of repetition does loom,
Anguished soul's bereavement cry, "My joy stole,"
Yet Christ died, once for all, sealing sin's doom;
Taking up all sorrows, sin to entomb,
Bearing every grief, Satan ne'er to troll.
Ever does sin exalt its head of gloom,
Yet Christ died, once for all, sealing sin's doom.

Opening this third cycle, the same villanelle that sealed sin's fate now seals the poet's bond with form—spiritual victory reborn as artistic mastery.

III.2

Love Rekindled

Rouse mute dormant yearnings unrequited,
Pause to tend feelings and nurture sacred space.
Love's secret garden, no longer hided,
Sweet caress in cherished place, invited,
Igniting passion in kindling embrace.
Rouse mute dormant yearnings unrequited,
Two fighting life's sharp thorns while divided:
Compassion cooled quickly in daily race.
Love's secret garden, no longer hided,
Awareness grows, tender blooms excited,
Blossoming oasis our hiding place.
Rouse mute dormant yearnings unrequited,
As blind spots are unseen, blindsided.
Sightlessness dulls awareness; yet deep grace,
Love's secret garden, no longer hided.
Loving touch, gentle embrace provided,
Entwined bond in our blessed marital place.
Rouse mute dormant yearnings unrequited,
Love's secret garden, no longer hided.

Marital renewal mirrors spiritual renewal; love's garden reopens, proving that sacred passion and poetic discipline bloom from the same soil.

III.3

Solitude's Fulfillment

Veiled solitude does silent vex belief,
Whispered aspersions sow freedom's discord,
Yet love's providence supplants hidden grief,
Transposes feeling, despair but made brief.
Surely delivered from brute's mindless horde:
Veiled solitude does silent vex belief,
Twisted passion obsessed souls become chief,
E'er shown wanting, life marred, blessings ignored.
Yet love's providence supplants hidden grief,
Gently woos, life renewed from virtue's thief,
Delivers from anxious bondage's ward.
Veiled solitude does silent vex belief,
Sparks awareness, fleeing ruthless barren fief,
Cruel towers, thrashing life-giving chord.
Yet love's providence supplants hidden grief,
Subsumes melancholy, brings relief
Of quavering nuptial embrace implored.
Veiled solitude does silent vex belief,
Yet love's providence supplants hidden grief.

Solitude vexes, yet providence relieves—the poet's pilgrimage from isolation to peace, from closed self to open faith.

III.4

Salvation's Sickness

Unceasing time's march quells weary aplomb
Ever driven to humility's bloom.
Unending devotion balms journey's tomb,
Quiet faithfulness walks abreast to whom
Fortuity lies—divinity's groom.
Unceasing time's march quells weary aplomb;
Tortured despair from barren lifeless womb—
Unspeakable grief—bewail empty room.
Unending devotion balms journey's tomb
While daily struggle with life's death fume
Yields inconsolable and heartless doom.
Unceasing time's march quells weary aplomb,
Fading youth and beauty silently loom,
Humanity despairs oncoming gloom.
Unending devotion balms journey's tomb
Where man's breath though fleeting is sweet perfume,
Life companion's love ever to illume
Unceasing time's march quells weary aplomb.
Unending devotion balms journey's tomb.

A rare villanelle in true monorhyme where every line echoes a single sound, letting form itself become the relentless march of time that devotion alone can balm.

III.5

Villanelle's Villanelle (An Ode to 'Nellie Villanelle)

Villanelle did accost my being whole,
Mind, spirit, reasoning: trembled, bound, failed.
Now 'Nellie enlightened my thoughts and soul,
To ponder well-worn paths, yield life's control,
Expand awareness, rhyme's mount all but scaled.
Villanelle did accost my being whole,
Confusion intruded, none to cajole,
Writing fled wounded and hopefulness paled.
Now 'Nellie enlightened my thoughts and soul,
Poem's promenade unbound, capriole
Reveals quest's end glimmer, triumph unveiled.
Villanelle did accost my being whole,
Vision wavered, unexpected knothole
Impeded perception, talent exhaled.
Now 'Nellie enlightened my thoughts and soul:
Opened heaven's gate, poet's pen console,
Liberated creative skills inhaled.
Villanelle did accost my being whole,
Now 'Nellie enlightened my thoughts and soul.

A meta-celebration of form as muse. The poet's struggle becomes revelation: constraint is not confinement but communion.

III.6

Not My Cup of Tea in Three Steps

I wrote a poem styled "Villanelle,"
And to this style I said, "Hucklebell!"

But then 'Nellie called, I wrote two more,
And to this style now cry, "Villadore!"

Now 'Nellie transcends my being whole;
She e're enlightens my thoughts and soul.

A playful epilogue; what began in mockery ends in affection—Nellie, once scorned, becomes the poet's beloved companion.

III.7

Deliverance of Form

Ponderous weight once squelched my soul,
Redeemed by rhyme's restraint.
Rhythmic lines now dost wax it full,
Form guides God's faint constraint.

A final echo uniting both arcs—grace and craft, faith and rhythm, fused as one liberation.

Coda

Seven turns of form become seven turns of freedom.
What once constrained now steadies; what once resisted now reveals.
Refrain by refrain, discipline becomes delight, and the poems breathe on their own terms.
The cycle closes in quiet mastery—grace and craft moving as one.

PART IV

Whimsy's Whetstone

A Poetic Cycle on the Knife-Edge of Play

Whimsy's Whetstone hones joy on the ordinary, sharpening the heart through play.
From beard to pie to noodle, each piece strikes a small spark—laughter not as distraction but as discipline's twin.
Emerging from form's rigor, the spirit here lightens without losing edge.

IV.1

Facial Foliage Fiasco

When e're my old man tried to hug us,
It always created a ruckus.
His beard being large,
'Bout the size of a barge,
Would smother and stifle and smush us.

A limerick of paternal affection gone comically awry; the rhyme snaps like a hug that won't let go.

IV.2

Pie Dilemma

I eat pie,
Goes to waist.
Don't eat it,
Landfill Waste.

Disappointed,
Both things bad.
And I think
I've been had.

Why cannot
I eat pie,
So that no
Tastebuds die?

"No," docs say,
"You must stop—
Every day—
Eating slop."

What burdens
I must bear,
while others
Do not care.

But these pains,
First world stuff,
don't matter—
I'll get buff.

A shaped quatrain ladder of temptation and resignation; the final twist—"I'll get buff"—turns guilt into grin.

IV.3

A Child's Wisdom

Said Kayleigh, age four or age five,
"You git what you git
and you don't throw a fit."
To this truth all people must strive.

A single quatrain distills toddler theology. The internal rhyme bounces like a child's shrug; wisdom arrives unannounced.

IV.4

Nonsense Natter

Babble, drivel, balderdash,
Jabber, jargon, duh-word-hash;
Chitting chatter and claptrap,
Yammer, prattle, nonsense-rap.

Mumbo jumbo, double talk,
Cadabra's word, magic crock;
Headless screed and hocus-thing,
Twaddle-pocus, language bling.

This the babble in my head,
Babble blabbers while in bed;
Blabbers rouse my thoughts anew,
Rouse's rabble, my soul askew.

A rollicking catalog of verbal nonsense. The four-beat lines pile like laundry; the final couplet turns inner chaos into comic confession.

IV.5

Instant Bliss

Oh I yearn for yummy chicken
Instant bliss ramen noodles. Rock
savory tastes, my heart quickens,
Instant bliss ramen noodles. Sock
each of my taste buds with becharmed
Instant bliss ramen noodles. Talk
sweetly and set my food alarm . . .
(Instant bliss ramen noodles) . . . clock.

An eight-line ode to instant comfort. The refrain repeats like a timer; the ellipsis is the moment the microwave dings.

Coda

Five sparks strike the edge: beard, pie, child, nonsense, noodle.
Laughter here is a blade that brightens, not a mask that hides.
Joy rises from the ordinary like a glint from stone—light, quick, and earned.
The heart leaves sharpened, not softened.

PART V

Quiet Epiphanies

A Poetic Cycle on the Still Small Voice

Quiet Epiphanies enters the stillness where the small, the plain, and the everyday crack open into grace.
These poems hinge on silence—soil, mind, sky, page—where revelation comes not through spectacle but subtlety.
Play's bright edge softens here into attentiveness, preparing the reader for deeper wrestling.

V.1

Time's Power

Excavating bit by bit,
On a slope afraid I'll slip,
All I have is my own wit,
So must rest and think a bit.

Much refreshed my mind now lit,
Coupled with enduring grit,
Double down then I must quit,
Else this hole becomes a pit.

Halfway done I now must knit,
Empty space with nature's kit,
Gently place as they befit,
Sprouts of providence's writ.

Nurture, cherish, ponder, sit:
Time's the silent player's skit.
Other things are but a whit,
Farmer's wisdom ne'er omit.

A sixteen-line meditation in monorhymed quatrains. Each four-line stanza digs deeper with relentless closure—time as patient farmer, not tyrant. The final stanza turns labor into providence.

V.2

Quietude

Full spaces depress
me, they get me down,
my head starts spinning;
All around

is confusion. When
I restrict hearing
the cacophony
taunt jeering,

solitude is
delightful. If
the thoughts of folks
creates a tiff

within your head,
that's spinning round,
to keep your mind,
tune inner sound.

A shaped stanza of narrowing lines. The form enacts retreat; the final couplet finds music in silence.

V.3

Look Up and Live

Body reclined, soul out of whack,
Release the tension from your back.
Take a deep breath and let it out,
To ponder what it's all about.

Is life consumed with just what's here,
With chattels all that we hold dear?
For this query, please look above;
There you'll find transcendent love.

Ask the Father's enlightenment,
He'll enable enlivenment:
Redeeming life from evil means,
As God in heaven truly deems.

Twelve measured lines in couplets. The gaze lifts from body to sky; grace descends in the asking.

V.4

Poetry's Provision

Oh how I love poetry,
It ever lets me be me.
'Tis a good thing all around:
Helps me keep my thoughts aground.

A quatrain coda. The cycle ends where it began—earthbound, grateful. Poetry anchors the epiphany.

Coda

Four small openings—soil, mind, sky, page—make room for quiet revelation.
Here silence becomes structure, and attention becomes prayer.
Nothing shouts; everything leans in.
The cycle rests in readiness: the spirit held steady, the ear newly awake.

PART VI

Daily Struggles

A Poetic Cycle on the Flesh's Quiet Wars

Daily Struggles returns to flesh and ground: the body's limits, the mind's loops, the ordinary resistances of life.
These poems trace the quiet wars—money, focus, age, obsession—where grace meets grit in the day-to-day.
From epiphany's hush, we step back into motion, carrying its clarity into conflict.

VI.1

Running's Problem Summation

While I seek the motivation
To run more, I'm on vacation
Too long, I seek extrication,
Running is then but cessation.

Rekindle running's causation,
Daily dwell on its cognation,
No, cognition my fixation,
I must stop each day's negation.

Problem is running's flirtation
Results in my mind's deflation,
So build with a sure foundation,
Don't waste time with mere gyration.

Now seek hard this germination,
Which then leads to true elation,
Not merely a fabrication
Brought about by self-inflation.

But I am bound by vexation,
Running's no more my vocation.
I must make mental translation,
Not allow running's truncation.

Is this fight but my tarnation,
Or is it only stagnation?
How to deal with this frustration?
Only speak baby dictation?

Solution's more that narration,
It comes down to ministration
Of the mind's true liberation—
Deliver running's salvation.

Seven monorhymed quatrains in unrelenting -ation, the obsession never once released—until "salvation" quietly turns the same sound from torment into mercy.

VI.2

Michelle's Split Focus

Sorry, sorry! I wasn't done.
Hubby and I are on the run
Rearranging the furniture,
Patio's better to be sure.

OK, I'm done, what do you want,
Grocery shopping? Hate to hunt.
We'll just stay here and sit around,
Let everyone else go to town.

Eight breezy lines. Domestic chaos in real time; the shrug is the struggle.

VI.3

Monetary Choices

Invest your money; live with the choice.
If it goes south and your eyes get moist,
Don't rant and rave for the pick you made,
Clash with folks as civility fades.

When these actions begin to happen
They react by block-button-slappin'.
There are better things to do today
Than to retort to cries of dismay,

Regret over not counting the cost,
Saying too quickly that all is lost.
Instead, build your credibility
By taking responsibility.

Twelve measured lines. The market's fall becomes a mirror for the heart.

VI.4

Defying Age

As I grow old
Fears do grow
That my running
Will grow slow
And my thinking
Grow slow too
Cold molasses
Just won't do
Life stays vibrant
This is how
Make each moment
In the now

A shaped stanza of descending then ascending lines. Age creeps; presence pushes back.

VI.5

Obsession's Freedom

Why does my mind obsess over thee?
Obsession snares freedom, yet I'm free.
Although obsessed, I am still not bound;
Mind energized, freedom truly found.

Why, then, daily does obsession bind,
Creating yearnings, compelling mind?
Is it bondage to new thoughts in me,
Or awareness of my freedom's glee?

Yes, my mind to freedom does obsess,
Every day seized my soul to possess,
Desire waxed full, enveloped by joy;
This sweet grace does give life to enjoy.

The villanelle's ghost haunts the refrain; obsession becomes offering.

Coda

Five skirmishes mark the day: running, clutter, money, age, obsession.
None end cleanly; all end standing.
Here grace is not the escape but the endurance—the stubborn joy that refuses to yield.
The cycle closes with breath enough for tomorrow.

Envoi

The circle widens: from first confession
to last refusal to be repaired.
Nothing settled, nothing left unsaid.
Wound, laugh, refrain—
The inward struggle echoing through every step—
and the page keeps walking with them.

APPENDIX A

The Six Cycles of Redemption

I - Sin's Remedy—Confession and Cleansing

Here, language bends under the weight of guilt and grace. Sin is exposed as both bondage and blindness, yet mercy remains the quiet antidote beneath every line. These poems reveal the fracture—and the healing—at the book's core.

II - AI-Yi-Yi!—Algorithm and Image

A reflection on technology as mirror and mimic. This cycle wrestles with the uncanny echo of human creativity within artificial systems, asking where the soul rests when language is replicated without breath.

III - The Form of Grace—Craft as Devotion

Poetic form becomes discipline, ritual, offering. Villanelle, monorhyme—each pattern is both structure and surrender. Grace becomes craft, and craft becomes worship.

IV - Whimsy's Whetstone—Joy as Sharpening

Laughter returns, not as escape but as refinement. Humor, lightness, and wordplay polish the spirit. Whimsy is revealed as sacred—joy as a tool of sanctification.

V - Quiet Epiphanies—Stillness and Seeing

The heart settles. These poems observe, receive, and rest. Insight emerges not through striving but through the hush that follows it. This is a cycle of gentle revelation.

VI – Daily Struggles—Battle and Breath

Where grace meets grit, and faith meets fatigue. These poems show the believer in the ring—wrestling doubt, distraction, obsession, and the endlessly human self. And yet: grace is the bell between rounds.

APPENDIX B

Redemptions

A Reader's Guide

I – Sin's Remedy

The redemption: You're drowning in sin's weight, then Christ exchanges his life for yours. The poem literally says "my vileness exchanged, my sin replaced." You go from "ponderous weight dost squelch my soul" to "ponderous grace dost wax it full." That's redemption—straight swap, death to life.

II – AI-Yi-Yi!

The redemption: The algorithm tries to kill your voice with its sterile perfection. You reclaim your breath. "Brash algorithm leads to poetry's death" but "Poet ponders breathing poem's life-breath." You refuse the machine and save poetry itself. Your human wit redeems art from code.

III – The Form of Grace

The redemption: The villanelle feels like a cage at first— "Villanelle did accost my being whole." But then you master it, and constraint becomes freedom. By the end: "Now 'Nellie enlightened my thoughts and soul." What bound you now liberates you. Discipline redeems creativity.

IV – Whimsy's Whetstone

The redemption: You stop taking everything so seriously. Laughter sharpens a dull soul. A kid's wisdom—"You git what you git and you don't throw a fit"—redeems your stressed-out mind. Joy rescues you from joylessness. Grace wears a grin.

V – Quiet Epiphanies

The redemption: Noise and chaos press in—"Full spaces depress me." Then you find stillness. "Look above; there you'll find transcendent love." Silence redeems the spinning mind. Listening saves you from the racket.

VI – Daily Struggles

The redemption: You're stuck in obsession, aging, procrastination—but you don't quit. "Obsession snares freedom, yet I'm free." You wrestle daily and keep showing up. Stubborn endurance redeems the grind. Grace isn't the knockout—it's staying in the ring.

Every part: Something binds you. Something frees you. That's redemption, six ways.

APPENDIX C

Blessing and Curse

The Pattern of Redemption

	Cycle *Name* Focus	*Curse* Bondage/ Constraint *Quote*	*Blessing* Freedom/Grace *Quote*	*Key Outcome/* *Redemption* *Quote*
I	*Sin's* *Remedy* The Soul	*Sin's Grip* Blindness, guilt, and human imperfection *Binds me tightly, yielding death to my soul* (I.2)	*Christ's Exchange* Atonement, forgiveness, and deliverance *Ponderous grace dost wax it full* (I.3)	*Grace* becomes *Doxology* *The good I should do, is Christ in me* (I.4)
II	*AI-Yi-Yi!* Poet/ Technol-ogy	*Algorithmic Mimicry* Code, mechani-cal precision *Brash algorithm leads to poetry's death* (II.3)	*Human Wit & Breath* Irony, satire, and the cadence of a living voice *Experience births from cauldron of time* (II.1)	*Discipline* be-comes *Defiance* *Can't do wordplay, thou blind mime* (II.4)
III	*The Form of Grace* Artist/ Craft	*Form's Constraint* The strict rules of the villanelle *Villanelle did accost my being whole* (III.5)	*Communion with Structure* Mastery turns con-straint into delight *Love's secret garden, no longer hided* (III.2)	*Grace* becomes *Craft* *Rhythmic lines now dost wax it full* (III.7)

	Cycle *Name* Focus	*Curse* Bondage/ Constraint *Quote*	*Blessing* Freedom/Grace *Quote*	*Key Outcome/* *Redemption* Quote
IV	*Whimsy's Whetstone* Heart/ Play	*Seriousness/ Dullness* Mental pressure, guilt over appetite, and inner chaos *Babble blabbers while in bed* (IV.4)	*Laughter & Play* Polishing joy on the ordinary, absurdity, and "comic confession" *You git what you git and you don't throw a fit* (IV.3)	*Grace* becomes *Laughter* *His beard being large, 'Bout the size of a barge* (IV.1)
V	*Quiet Epiphanies* Spirit/ Contemplation	*Noise/Activity* External chaos, and time as a tyrant *Full spaces depress me* (V.2)	*Silence & Listening* Stillness, retreat, and listening for the "still small voice" *There you'll find transcendent love* (V.3)	*Grace* becomes *Silence* *Time's the silent player's skit* (V.1)
VI	*Daily Struggles* Self/ Endurance	*Flesh's Quiet Wars* Physical aging, obsession, procrastination, and financial worries *Running is then but cessation* (VI.1)	*Wry Tenacity* Stubborn joy, endurance, and finding grace in the wrestle *Obsession snares freedom, yet I'm free* (VI.5)	*Grace* becomes *Stubborn Joy* *Life stays vibrant This is how Make each moment In the now* (VI.4)

The overarching message is that true *freedom is found when surrender refines the will*, and this transformation is experienced through all six dimensions.

Note on Terms

Atonement—Christ's exchange of His righteousness for our sin, reconciling us to God.

Coda—a concluding passage that gathers the cycle's threads, offering rest without full closure.

Couplet—two successive rhyming lines, often used to close a thought with a sudden click of recognition.

Doxology—a brief expression of praise to God, often marking the turn from struggle to gratitude.

Envoi—a short stanza sending off the work, often with a nod to its intent or recipient.

Epigram—a concise, witty statement that distills truth with a twist.

Form—in both poetry and faith, the accepted limits through which true freedom is discovered.

Freedom—not the absence of constraint, but harmony between necessity and will.

Grace—the unearned gift by which both life and art are set free.

Hinge poem—a spare piece that pivots the sequence, turning lament toward grace with a single breath.

Lament—an honest outpouring of sorrow, the soul's cry that grace quietly answers.

Limerick—a five-line humorous form with an AABBA rhyme scheme, light but structured.

Monorhyme—a poem or stanza in which every line ends on the same rhyme sound.

Ode—a lyric celebration of a subject, turning the mundane into something sung.

Quatrain—a four-line stanza, the quiet workhorse of English hymnody and complaint.

Redemption—deliverance from any bondage through mercy and transformation.

Shaped poem—a poem whose visual arrangement on the page participates in its meaning.

Sin—the will's turning from divine order, healed only by grace.

Spare poem—a piece deliberately thinned to bone so that every remaining word rings like struck flint.

Villanelle—a nineteen-line form built on two refrains and two repeating rhymes.

www.ingramcontent.com/pod-product-compliance
Lightning Source LLC
LaVergne TN
LVHW010542100826
845148LV00013B/2570
9798385271207